A TO Z OF ART FOR KIDS

AGATA AND PIERRE TOROMANOFF

TO OUR NEWBORN
DAUGHTER EMILIE

A to Z

OF

ART

FOR KIDS

EKEN
PRESS

TABLE OF CONTENTS

ABSTRACTION

In art, abstraction is a play of forms, shapes, and colors that does not represent anything we know from reality. Abstract images do not refer to concrete objects or persons; rather they evoke emotions and speak to our imagination. Abstract art can consist of geometric forms placed together, or it can be even more spontaneous – an artist may follow his hand's movement and inspiration to create forms on the canvas, a little bit as if he was painting while dreaming.

You can have abstract drawings, paintings, photographs, or sculptures. Abstract art emerged at the beginning of the 20th century and has been an important mode of artistic expression since then. The opposite is realism.

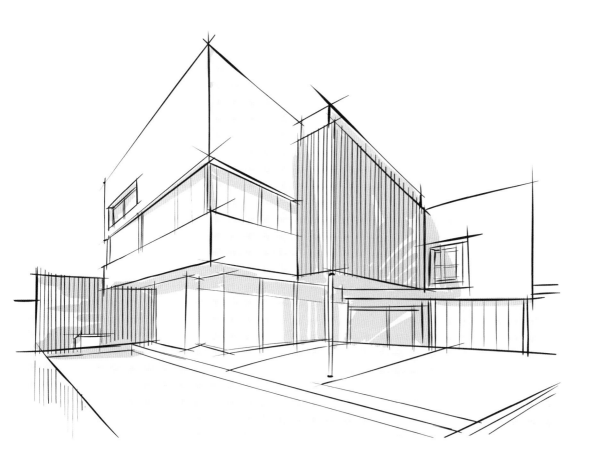

ARCHITECTURE...

Architecture is the art of sketching and constructing buildings, both outside and inside. When you build a house with LEGO® bricks, a hut in the garden, or a sand castle on the beach, you act like an architect. Architecture is an important element in our everyday life, as we use buildings to live, learn, play, or travel. Think about a farmhouse, a skyscraper, and an airport: all these buildings are elements of architecture, along with schools, hospitals, factories, or churches. All of them vary in size and style and are adapted to their purpose; a good building must be both beautiful and functional so that people feel comfortable in it.

...ARCHITECTURE

The materials used to construct them are carefully selected by architects: it may be bricks, stones, wooden panels, tiles, fabrics, plaster, concrete, steel, or glass. Buildings are also adapted to the climate and their geographical location: in warm countries, they must protect people from the heat, in cold regions from the low temperatures. A house on the seaside will look different from a house in the mountains, just like there is a difference between countryside and city architecture. All buildings must comply with safety regulations and should be environment-friendly. Some are very original in their shapes; others look more traditional and less eye-catching.

ARTIST

An artist is a creative person with a lot of talent and imagination. By painting, sculpting, drawing, or photographing, artists express their vision of the surrounding world and their feelings, which they want to share with others. Artists use various media, tools and techniques to create artworks. A painter will need a canvas and paint, a sculptor a stone, a photographer a camera and light, etc. Artists have to learn and train to get the best from their skills. Some artists work across media and create complex works using several tools and techniques.

ARTWORK

An artwork, or in other words a work of art, results from an artist's imagination and creative practice. It expresses ideas, emotions, or stories in an artistic form. If it is an image painted on a canvas, it is a painting. If it is a three-dimensional object, it is a sculpture.

BOOKS

Books are an important way of learning about art but also enjoying it. Books on art can present various artists who lived and worked at the same period of time, an artist's work throughout his or her life, or simply a theme in art. Lavishly illustrated, art books not only feature various artworks but also include texts written by experts who know a lot about the artists and the subject. This is the way you learn what the artworks look like, see details you may not spot otherwise, and discover more about the story behind them – when and where they were created, the idea that inspired it, or who the artist was.

BEAUTY

We tend to call something beautiful when it pleases our eyes. Beautiful artworks are generally harmonious – the colors, shapes, and proportions promote a feeling of harmony and elegance. Beauty is difficult to describe precisely because everyone has their own perception and definition of beauty. Over the centuries, the idea of beauty has often changed according to the zeitgeist, or the trends and fashions of the time. Artworks reflect the perception of beauty as mirrors of their times.

C

COLLAGE

A collage is an assemblage of various elements or pieces that altogether form an artwork. In a collage, elements like photographs, drawings, pieces of newspapers, parts of some objects, or fabrics are cut out and arranged in an original composition. The pieces interlock a bit like in a puzzle, but less orderly. A collage can include three-dimensional elements and look like a sculpture.

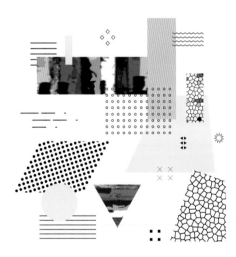

COLLECTION

An art collection is a group of artworks collected over time either by an individual collector, an art lover, or an institution like a museum. A private collection is created according to someone's taste and is rarely open for public viewing. By contrast, a public collection gathered by a museum is accessible to a wide audience in order to present a heritage of the arts. It is created by specialists and preserves historical or contemporary artworks. Collections can be organized into various categories like medium, period of time the artworks were created in, theme, or artists.

COLOR

Technically, a color is the result of how an object reflects light. The intensity of light makes the perception of colors vary. There are three primary colors: yellow, red, and blue. By mixing them together we get a range of secondary colors:

yellow + red = orange   red + blue = violet   blue + yellow = green

This is the spectrum of colors you can see in a rainbow.
Further combinations will make any other hue.

Colors matter because they help us spot objects, but also because they are associated with memories and emotions: red, for example, is the color of blood and fire; it is associated with energy, life, and strength. Green is the color of nature and freshness. The yellow of the sun reminds us of joy, happiness, and energy. Colors are used in art to create an atmosphere or to form a contrast.

COMPOSITION

The way an artist arranges various elements within a work of art is called *composition*. The artist creates a scene with elements of different sizes, colors, and shapes, some being in the front, others in the back. Also, the light is part of a composition, be it in a painting, a photograph, or a sculpture.

A composition can be
HARMONIC when it gives the feeling that all elements are in the right places.
DISSONANT when it is as if the elements were mixed like the pieces of a jigsaw puzzle.
STATIC when it gives the feeling that things are immobile, as if frozen in time.
DYNAMIC, as if the elements were moving.
SYMMETRIC when top and bottom, right and left sides of the composition are balanced.
ASSYMETRIC when it is unbalanced, with all elements on one side of the composition.

CONCEPTUAL ART

When the idea or the message expressed in an artwork is more important than the composition itself, it is considered conceptual art. Conceptual art gives the message or the ideas expressed by the artist precedence over the artistic qualities of the work, a little bit like in advertising. The aim of conceptual art is to invite the viewer to think about what the artist meant and to engage in a dialogue with the artwork.

CONTRAST

A contrast arises when two completely different or even opposite shapes, colors, or materials are placed next to each other, thus emphasizing their differences. Black and white or big and small are the most usual contrasts. Materials like wood and glass, or features like static and dynamic, usually provide a feeling of contrast. One composition can consist of several contrasting elements.

CRAFT

In the arts, craft is the making of objects such as furniture. Imagine a carpenter crafting a wooden table with his bare hands. The activity requires extensive experience developed in training, but also skill. Today many objects are mass-produced by machines in factories. In the past, things were handmade by craftsmen in their workshops in limited numbers, which resulted in high quality and unique objects. Nowadays more and more people are returning to craft and work by hand because craft equals constructing with care and precision and using the best materials.

CURATOR

A curator is a person who is in charge of organizing temporary exhibitions (at galleries or museums, for example) or who looks after an existing collection of artworks in a museum or for a private art collector. This activity requires a wide knowledge of art and artists. Curators of temporary exhibitions must display the artworks so that visitors are gradually introduced into the artists' work and can navigate from one piece to another. Curators looking after permanent collections are tasked with acquiring new artworks that increase and enrich the collection.

DECORATION

Artworks can be also used to decorate spaces by creating a particular atmosphere. An artwork, especially one representing a lovely landscape or a bunch of flowers, can decorate a wall it hangs on. A painting, sculpture, photograph, or poster are possible decorative elements in a bedroom or a living room. You can find artworks at many public spaces: gardens, train stations, and hotel hallways and lobbies, for example. You can also decorate a wall or a whole building by covering them with decorative elements (a colorful wallpaper, a fresco featuring some scene, or an interesting pattern).

DESIGN

In our everyday life, we use various objects. You use an alarm clock to wake up, plates and cutlery to eat your breakfast, your bike or the school bus to go to school. Actually, everything you're surrounded by is sketched and then created by designers, who have to create objects that are not only easy to use but also pleasant for the eye: think about smartphones, watches, shoes, or furniture. Their form and the way they function has to be well adjusted to their roles, so the design process requires thinking out of the box and knowledge about various materials, and also users' needs.

DETAIL

Each artwork, regardless of medium, consists of various elements. These elements form the whole, but individually they are all very important. That is precisely why, when looking at an artwork, we should pay particular attention to the details. Even the tiniest ones can be very interesting or simply helpful in understanding and appreciating the artwork.

DESTINATION

In the past, artworks were created exclusively on commission. When wealthy people acting as patrons of art wished to commemorate important events or to decorate their interiors, they asked a painter or a sculptor to create a work of art – it could be a portrait of the person, a landscape they particularly like, or a sculpture of a famous hero. Today you can see historical artworks in various museums, but they were originally created for churches, royal residences, or other palaces. In the early 19th century artists started creating artworks just to express their vision of beauty, without thinking about where the artwork would be housed, although even nowadays it is not uncommon for institutions, galleries, or art lovers to commission artworks from artists.

DRAWING

You know exactly what a drawing is. I am sure you like drawing many things you see around you. In art, it is a technique artists use to produce either a final artwork or a preparatory sketch. Painters, sculptors, or architects often first sketch their ideas before they move on to work on paintings, sculptures, or buildings. Depending on the materials used – pencil, crayons, ink, charcoal, or chalk – each drawing will look a bit different. Even if a drawing depicts lines, these materials allow the showing of various tones and perspectives.

EDUCATION

Far back in the past, the best way to become an artist was to join the workshop of a famous artist and to train under the artist's supervision and learn from the artist. Today, some artists graduate art schools, while others are self-taught artists. In the first case the art education is thorough and lasts several years. In the second one, the educational process is based on personal research and examining the art of the past as well as extensive practice. In both cases learning about the past and mastering various techniques give a good start for developing one's own artistic career.

EPOCHS

Art has evolved over the centuries, from decorated artifacts, sculptures, and frescoes by cavemen and masterpieces from ancient Egypt through to contemporary art, which refers to living artists. Just like history is divided into periods, artworks are usually classified according to the time and place they were created. Each epoch can be identified by characteristic features: one can easily differentiate a masterpiece by a Native American artist from a sculpture dating to the Italian Renaissance, or a traditional Japanese woodprint from a painting by a contemporary abstract painter.

EXHIBITION

An exhibition is a presentation of artworks. It is organized by a curator on behalf of a museum or a gallery, or for an art event. An exhibition can be dedicated to one artist in particular or an artistic group, an epoch or a movement of art (Renaissance or Impressionism), or a specific sub-ject (British sculpture). Organizing an exhibition requires renting works from various museums and collections to bring them into one place. If it's a presentation of a living artist, they are also invited to take part in the process. Sometimes artists create works especially for a particular exhibition. Some exhibitions have a catalog in the form of a printed book with photos of works from the show as well as essays on the subject.

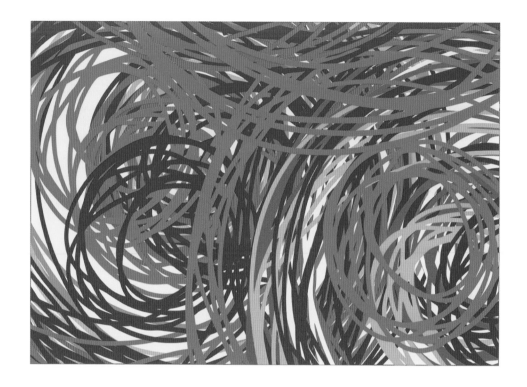

EXPRESSION

Art is the way of looking at and representing the world around us. Creating an artwork means expressing how one perceives and understands the world. Each artwork is an expression of emotions and reflections, which we can compare with ours – just like music can reflect our emotions, feelings, and states of mind. Sometimes we say that an artwork is particularly expressive, which means that it is meaningful and iconic.

EVENTS

The art world has museums with impressive collections all over the globe, sculpture parks in many cities of the world, and art galleries presenting numerous exhibitions. In addition to these permanent displays of artworks, temporary artistic events are organized regularly and gather crowds of art fans. Art fairs (in the photo) are among them. They take place in various cities all year round. Collectors and museum directors can purchase new artworks for their collections. There are also Biennales – events happening every two years, the most popular of which takes place in Venice. Some cities like Berlin or Copenhagen organize art weeks or art weekends with lots of special shows and attractions. Others host big art festivals.

World News

FAME

An artist is famous when her or his works are exhibited around the globe. How to become a famous artist? First of all, an artist must be innovative in what he or she creates, secondly his or her style should be distinguishable from others. Some artists are remembered in history for groundbreaking innovations that influenced the following generations of artists. In the past fame spread more slowly than nowadays, as artists had to travel in person from country to country to show their work. Today, the Internet and modern means of transportation make it much easier and quicker.

FASHION

Fashion, the art of designing and creating clothes, also belongs to the creative industry and more than ever is close to the visual arts. People who create clothes are called fashion designers and work for various fashion brands. They invent new cuts and set new trends. Inspired by various sources, including art, they dictate what is currently in fashion and how we should dress. Sometimes the brands decide to work directly with artists who either use their artworks as patterns for the clothes and accessories or design something special. Fashion shows are organized to popularize a new collection of clothes. Models wear new designs on a catwalk surrounded by an audience. The clothes are also photographed by photographers specializing in shooting fashion. Fashion photography is then published in magazines and books.

FILM

French visionaries, the Lumière brothers, invented the first ever cinematograph, or motion picture camera, at the end of the 19th century. Before them, the only possibility was to take a single image - a photograph. The brothers' idea was to collect a series of still images and show them in sequence. Imagine for example someone walking and photos showing each step. When you look at these photos one after another very quickly, you will have a feeling you see the person in the image moving. That's how the first films were created. You can do the same with drawings to make an animated movie. Today the technology and cameras are much more advanced, and many visual effects are done with the help of a computer.

GALLERY

At first glance, a gallery looks like a small-size museum. However, galleries tend to organize shows more frequently than museums, and they usually do not have a permanent collection, as they only have temporary exhibitions for their audience. Some galleries are focused on one medium, like photography or sculpture. They offer educational activities to help children, and adults, discover art. There are also galleries in major cities that not only present artists within temporary exhibitions but also sell their works. Galleries are worth visiting on a regular basis to learn more about emerging artists.

GLASS

Forming objects out of glass is another kind of art. The technique is called glassblowing and uses a blowpipe, which helps inflate molten glass into a bubble. This way you can produce lamps or vases, among other things. There is also a very special kind of glass that is colored. It has a long history and is called stained glass. Small pieces of glass in various forms and colors are arranged to form a picture or a decorative pattern and are connected with strips of lead. Stained glass is most common in windows (you may have seen it in churches or other buildings). When the sun shines, the colorful compositions are beautifully illuminated.

GRAPHIC DESIGN

One of the branches of design is graphic design, which combines photography, illustration, and typography (the way the letters look like when printed). Pages of magazines, newspapers, and books; the packaging of various objects; posters or leaflets; the look of a website; and the logos you recognize various companies by are all created by graphic designers. Their projects have to be communicative and easy to understand but also interesting visually. If there is a poster on a wall, it should catch your attention with an interesting composition, and you should quickly understand what it is about.

HISTORY

When you look back at many centuries of the world's art, the past will look like a fascinating story. Across time, continents, and various cultures, many people created art. It has changed over the centuries together with technical and cultural progress. It is fascinating to learn how new materials improved architecture or innovative techniques contributed to new trends in painting. Each moment in history has its specific character, which is reflected in the artworks of that time. Each artist adds an interesting aspect to history through his or her life, talent, and creation. History is also often a subject of art. Artists illustrate crucial past events or make artworks inspired by them.

ILLUSTRATION

This comes from the word illustrate – to give something a visual form. In a book, for example, illustrations show what the text tells about. Illustration not only has an informative role, it also gives pleasure to the eye to have some drawings or paintings (these are the most common techniques) to accompany or sometimes explain the reading, especially if they are colorful. People who create illustrations for books or magazines are called illustrators. In the past, they drew the illustrations by hand or etched them on plates. Nowadays they use computers to create and design the illustrations. You will also see illustrations on posters, video games, and various flyers.

IMAGINATION

What you see with your eyes is one thing, but you can also use your imagination to see even more. Let's say you draw a park. You can draw simple paths and trees and grass. But if you let your imagination run free, you will add colorful flowers, various animals, people walking, or even a pond. With a bit of imagination, you will invent many details to show a park in an interesting way. Artists have a naturally creative and fertile imagination. They use it whenever they wish to create artwork that accurately expresses their vision and is original at the same time.

INSPIRATION

To create original works, an artist needs not only imagination but also inspiration – it's like the fuel for the car; without it, it simply won't drive. Getting inspired means finding new ideas or subjects for their work. Artists travel, read books, talk to various people, learn about new cultures, or contemplate artworks created by other artists to find inspiration.

INSTALLATION

Paintings, sculptures, and photographs are all traditional artworks, but that doesn't mean they are the only ones. An installation, for example, is a large construction made of various elements that form an artwork; the idea is not to create a single piece of art, but rather to make the audience plunge into the atmosphere created by the installation. It can be a play of mirrors and lights, or something associating music and colors. Generally, the viewers can walk around it or even through it depending on the artist's concept. This interaction can be fun and evokes a lot of emotions.

INTERPRETATION

How you interpret an artwork is how you understand it. Generally, artists name their artworks, and the name gives us a hint about what they want to show. Sometimes the works are untitled, and we are free to imagine what the artist meant to represent, a bit like a riddle. What you see and feel is most important in understanding a piece of art.

INVENTIONS

Just as in any other field of human knowledge, inventions are very important in art, as they move everything forward and make beautiful things happen. At the end of the 19th century, for example, paints started being available in tubes. It seems normal now (we all use paints in tubes), but before that artists had to prepare the paints themselves and keep them on a wooden palette in their studios. Ready-mix paints in a tube are easy to carry, which allows artists to leave the confines of their studios and paint in nature, where light is much different and you can paint what you see in front of you, thus finding direct inspiration in nature.

JOKE

Art does not need to be very serious or boring. On the contrary, many artists have a great sense of humor. Even if they want to draw our attention to an important subject, they often do it in a playful way. Either they play with forms and sizes or with the original meanings. An interesting artwork will make you think, but it can also make you laugh or at least smile.

KINETIC ART

When we think about an artwork, we normally think about a static object. A painting or a photograph on the wall, a sculpture or an installation do not move. However, artists like breaking rules. Some of them, inspired by the forces of nature as well as modern machines, wished to make artworks move. Kinetic art was invented in the 20th century and is used mainly in sculptures that are mechanically supported or built so that the air can set their elements in motion. There are artists who try to achieve the effect of motion in two-dimensional mediums like paintings through optical illusion.

LAND ART

Can you imagine a work of art in the form of a gigantic island built by an artist of earth on water? This is possible only in the world of art! Land art with its artworks made by playing with the landscape was one of the movements of the 20th century, but many artists are still inspired by nature today. Some of them bring natural materials into galleries and open spaces to create unusual installations for visitors to enjoy or to draw attention to important environmental issues affecting our planet.

LANDSCAPE

Until the 17th century, landscapes were often used by artists only as a background for various scenes. Then the landscape became an individual genre of art. A painting representing a landscape in the countryside, the seaside, or in the mountains is seen as a tribute to the beauty of nature or a way to immortalize a particular place. Although some landscapes are created in studios, most landscape artists paint outdoors, which allows them to look directly at the view they are depicting.

Landscapes can show actual places, but also imaginary ones. In some paintings both the real and imaginary are mixed. As soon as the camera was invented, landscapes became a subject of photography too. If a photographer wants to show an imaginary landscape (or mix it with the real one), today they use computers and transform the images digitally by combining various elements of different photos into one. To give the best idea of a view, landscapes usually have horizontal formats.

LIGHT

Without light, we would not be able to see anything. Light is just as important as water and air for life. In art, light is an essential element of composition. In paintings or photographs, a specific kind of light is often used to create a particular atmosphere – of joy, warmth, or mystery, for example. Stained glass windows , which allow light to go through, can best be seen when they are illuminated by a ray of light.

LOOK

Looking at artworks is a great way to exert your observational skills. Without hurry, and with attention and curiosity, look first at the artwork as a whole, then you can try to catch details that are not visible at first glance. You will understand how the artists composed their works and what makes an artwork similar to reality or, on the contrary, completely different from what one usually perceives. If it is a piece of modern art, such as an installation, you will use not only your eyes, but also other senses, although touching art-works is usually not permitted.

MASTERS

We call some particularly important artists "masters," whose skills, talent, and unique style have inspired many generations of artists and whose fame has remained high over the centuries. They are just like great historical personalities or famous writers. In the history of art, the word *master* is mainly used for painters who lived and worked in the period between 1500 and 1800. Leonardo da Vinci, Michelangelo, Rembrandt (in the photo), and Dürer are the most famous masters, but there are many other masters of art to discover, and some particularly influential contemporary painters are considered masters as well.

MEDIUM

Medium refers to a type of art, like painting, sculpture, or photography. Actually, each kind of artwork is automatically its medium. Usually artists select one medium for their creation, but some decide not to specialize and work across several media. The second meaning of the word is the artistic material used to create an artwork, like paint in painting or clay in sculpture.

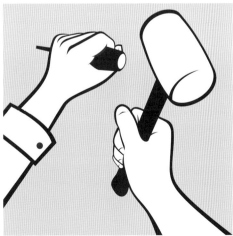

MOVEMENTS

When artists are interested in the same subjects, or when they share the same vision and use similar techniques, they usually form a group, which in time becomes an art movement or a milestone in the history of art. In the 19th century, for example, a handful of young painters decided that they wanted to render the emotional atmosphere of the scenes they depicted rather than the exact lines and contours. They were subsequently called "impressionists" (in the photo below) because

their subjective impressions were more important that the precise, photographic depiction of reality. The impressionist movement is now considered one of the foregoers of modern art. Surrealism, which combines reality and fantasy in illogical or absurd compositions, is another well-known movement (in the photo above), just like abstractionism, or abstract art.

MUSEUM

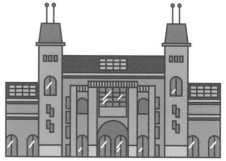
Rijksmuseum

An art museum is an institution that displays and preserves works of art of all kinds and is open to the public. Usually housed in large buildings that can accommodate spacious exhibition rooms, storage and maintenance facilities, a library, and services for visitors, museums offer two kinds of exhibitions planned by curators:

• The permanent collection is a selection of artworks from the museum's treasures, which can be arranged either chronologically or by themes.
• Temporary shows, organized several times a year, feature works by a particular artist or are dedicated to works created during a specific epoch, or present the art of a particular region or theme.

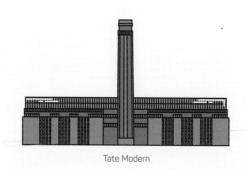
Tate Modern

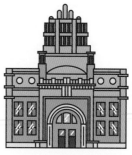
Victoria and Albert Museum

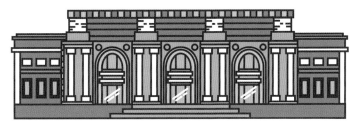
Metropolitan Museum of Art

Many museums have large permanent collections and keep buying new artworks to renew and enrich their vaults. They therefore need a team specializing in the storage and maintenance of artworks, to conserve them in good condition and to restore them if they are damaged.

Big cities host some of the most prestigious and large museums. There are also smaller, but no less interesting, museums in other cities and towns around the globe. You can find art museums presenting historical collections and others dedicated to modern and contemporary art. Also, some houses where famous painters and sculptors lived are transformed into museums.

Interestingly, museums are sometimes established by wealthy private collectors who invite the public to look at their art collections. Private collectors team up with famous architects to build new venues, unless they decide to display the works in their own homes.

Museo del Prado

Louvre Museum

NATURE

One of the main sources of inspiration for artists, architects, designers, and all creative people is nature. Careful observations of animals, plants, and landscapes result in copying their shapes, ornamental elements, or colors. A vase can be inspired by the shape of a lake; a ceiling in a building can mimic the form of waves on the water. The natural world is a great source of patterns too. In many art pieces, nature becomes the main subject, like in landscape painting. Some modern artists also try to recreate natural elements such as waterfalls, caves, or climatic conditions to draw attention to environmental issues or offer a surprising experience to the viewers. The most direct interaction of artists and nature is called land art.

OUTDOOR ART

Art does not only belong in museums or private homes. Art-works, usually sculptures, can also be displayed in public, open-air spaces like streets, gardens, or squares. Their location and shape interplay with the surrounding elements in interesting ways, either to complement the space or to intrigue the pass-erby. Some artists use unique materials or specific colors, while others create works of spectacular size and of surprising forms. As weather conditions may damage them, outdoor artworks must be made of long-lasting materials. All around the globe there are also sculpture parks with extensive areas devoted exclusively to displaying sculptures. The idea is to walk around and experience new shapes and concepts from each work. Street art is another popular kind of outdoor art.

OP ART

Op art stands for "optical art." It uses geometric forms and color contrasts to create an illusion of movement or a three-dimensional effect in artworks. It plays with what our eye perceives and analyzes, just like other optical illusions. Dynamic compositions, often in black and white, use the relationship between the background and foreground, or the perspective, to produce a feeling of movement. We can see alternately different shapes, or the image seems to vibrate in front of our eyes. Op art was invented in the 1960s, and its effects have been used by many artists across all major art mediums since then. Most of these powerful artworks are abstract, but some use elements we know perfectly to challenge the way we look at objects in space.

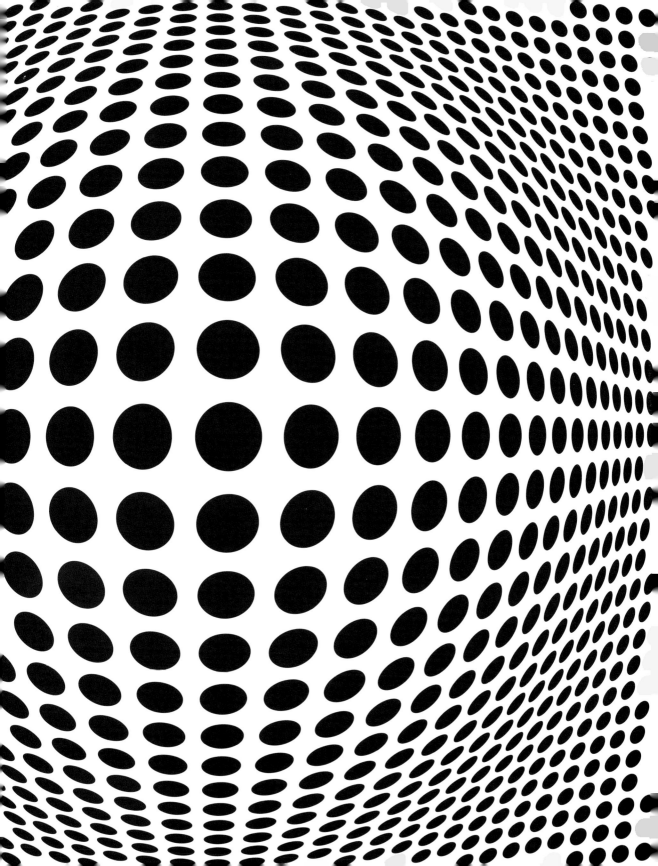

PAINTING

Painting is among the most dominant and the oldest of the artistic media. We use the same word to speak about the result of the artistic activity of applying paint to a support (surface). So, a painting = paint + base, and there are many kinds of paints and various types of support bases. The oldest paintings were painted on fabrics and wood. Then around the 16th century artists started to paint on canvases stretched and fixed to wooden frames. Another common surface is paper or fabric.

Paint consists of colored powders, called pigments, which are dissolved usually in oil or an acrylic emulsion (in the past egg was also used to bind the pigments). The pigments used to be produced from natural sources such as minerals or plants. Nowadays, most of them are synthetic and are produced through chemical processes. There are many kinds of paint: tempera, oil, acrylic, pastel, and watercolor. The selection of paint depends on the surface that is used as well as the result the artist wishes to obtain, as each paint has different qualities.

PATTERN

If you think about wallpaper in a room or the fabric a sofa is covered in or a T-shirt, you may notice that many of them have repeating shapes, colors, or lines on their surfaces. When this arrangement is regular, we call it a pattern. Patterns can be applied to many objects, featured in paintings or photographs, or be a decorative part of a building. They can repeat floral elements as well as geometric forms (or both). Actually, any image that is designed in a regular and repetitive way is a pattern.

PERFORMANCE

Performance is an artistic form that was born in the 20th century. The idea is that an artist or a group of them perform actions in front of an audience, just like singers or comedians onstage. Performance art can happen in a gallery or any other space. With their movements, as well as carefully selected activities and objects, artists make their art live – performances are, in a way, animated art. Sometimes they also involve the audience, which is invited to take part in the performance. A performance is usually seen by a small group of people, but they are recorded to be shown to a wider audience. This is quite different from static art, like painting or sculpture, and it is close to dance or theater.

“

PERSPECTIVE

Two-dimensional works, like paintings, are flat (they only have length and height), so there is difficulty in representing objects that are supposed to be closer to or farther away from the front of the painting, or simply in showing space. Centuries ago painters invented a way to overcome this difficulty. It is called perspective – a composition of straight lines arranged at particular angles to create an illusion of depth.

PHOTOGRAPHY

Nowadays, many people take pictures with their smartphones every time they see something interesting. Photography is part of our everyday life. But when it was invented in the 19th century, it was a revelation. People could take photographs of places and people to keep the memory of them (before that, the only way to capture anything was to draw it or paint it). At first, not many people could afford cameras, but thanks to ever-improving technology, photography has become a very popular pastime.

When you take a picture with a camera, an image is produced by the light interacting with a light-sensitive material. Initially, photography was non-digital, so you needed a light-sensitive film inside the camera that was later developed and reproduced on paper through a chemical process. Today most photographers use digital cameras, so the photos are stored in the camera's memory and can be easily transferred to a computer or simply printed. While the non-digital images could not be changed without a delicate and rather complicated retouching process, digital photos can be easily transformed and retouched with special computer programs.

69

PORTRAIT

A portrait is a painting of someone done so that you can easily recognize the person. Now we can easily take pictures with a camera, but remember that in the past there were no cameras, so people had to pose (often for many hours) for painters who tried to capture their appearance as precisely as possible. Portraits were commissioned by members of noble families or kings. Sometimes artists had to paint group portraits too, of a couple, family, society, or brotherhood. Portraits often idealized an individual and made them look more heroic or more beautiful than in real life. A painting in which an artist paints her- or himself is called a self-portrait.

71

PRINTMAKING

Have you ever played with rubber stamps? Printmaking is the same, but for artworks. Making pictures or patterns by printing them on paper or any other surface from specially prepared plates or blocks is called printmaking. It is an old artistic practice, which can be found mainly in Europe and Japan. The plates can be made of metal, stone, or wood. Artists carve an image on the plate using tools adequate for the material they are made of. Afterward the plate is covered with ink, which is transferred to paper or any other material. The final result – the print – is usually made in a limited number of copies.

PROPORTION

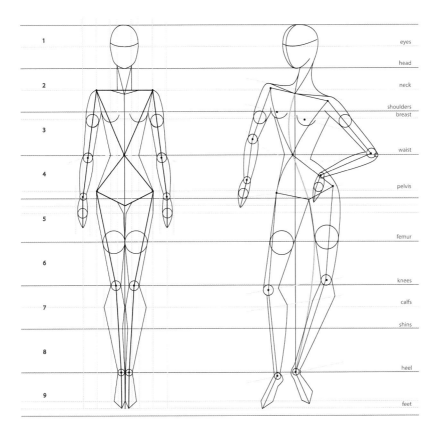

A good artwork must reflect the respective size of all elements that comprise it. If they are at the same level, an elephant cannot look smaller than a cat, for example, otherwise the artwork would not look harmonious. In the case of a human portrait, the hands cannot be longer than the legs, or the eyes bigger than the mouth. Sometimes artists purposely play with proportions and distort them to draw our attention to something or to put the emphasis on a part of the composition.

QUESTIONS

Discovering and enjoying artworks is an exciting adventure.
Always look closely and attentively at any kind of artistic
creation. Imagine you are playing a detective solving
a puzzle by initiating a conversation with an artwork,
which may include the following questions:

WHAT CATCHES YOUR EYE?

WHAT DO YOU THINK IT IS ABOUT?

DOES IT REMIND YOU OF ANYTHING YOU KNOW?

IS THERE ANY COLOR OR SHAPE THAT STANDS OUT?

WHAT IS ACTUALLY HAPPENING IN THE WORK?

IS ANYTHING SIMILAR TO ACTUAL OBJECTS YOU KNOW?

DOES IT TELL A STORY? WHAT IS THE SUBJECT?

IS THERE ANY INTERESTING DETAIL YOU HAVE NOTICED?

WHAT MATERIALS AND TECHNIQUES ARE USED?

WHAT IS THE SCALE OF THE WORK?

WHERE IS IT LOCATED?

DO YOU FIND HARMONY OR RHYTHM
IN THE COMPOSITION?

IF THERE IS A TITLE, DO YOU THINK IT
MATCHES THE WORK?

HOW DOES IT MAKE YOU FEEL? ARE YOU
BORED, EXCITED, INTERESTED?

Feel free to invent some additional ones.
Remember, the more question marks, the more answers!

REALISM

We call an artwork realist when a painting or a sculpture looks as if the artist was depicting exactly what he saw, without adding any special effects. Some portraits, for example, are so real that you can imagine the person speaking to you or moving inside the frame.

SCALE

Scale is simply the size of an artwork. Both painting and photography are generally small-scale works, but sculpture or installations can vary greatly in size. Large-scale projects are usually located outdoors. It is always good to check how the scale influences the way we look at an artwork. In many cases artists play with traditional sizes and either enlarge or minimize compositions to challenge the way we understand them.

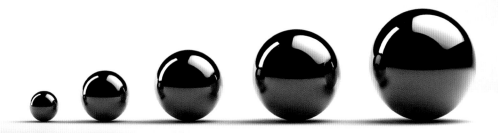

SCULPTURE

A sculpture is a three-dimensional piece of art that can be carved (when you have to remove material), modeled, welded (when you join material together with heat) or cast (when you make a form and fill it with material that has been melted at high temperatures). There are many materials a sculpture can be made of, such as marble, stone, metal, wood, aluminum, or clay, to name but a few. It can show realistic elements, even if in unusual proportions, or consist of abstract shapes. The scale of a sculpture varies depending on the destination and subject. An artist who creates sculptures is called a sculptor.

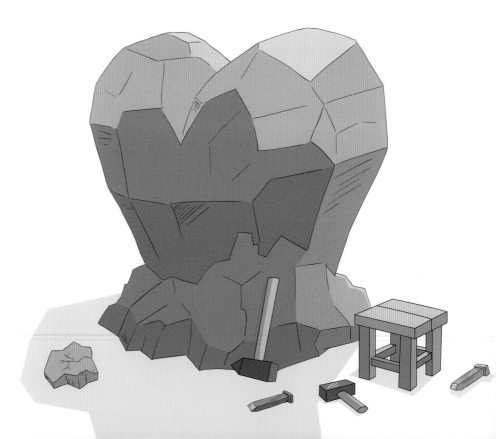

SPACE

Imagine a room. All of what is between the walls, the ceiling, and the floor is space. If there are any pieces of furniture in the room, they are standing in the space. Space is an empty and transparent area around everything that exists. We experience it naturally by simply being in an open outdoor space or an interior. Two-dimensional artworks like painting or drawing show space using perspective. Three-dimensional works, like sculptures or installations, exist in space.

STORY

Many artworks, although not all of them, are created to tell a story. In one work or a series of works we can see characters experiencing adventures, a bit like in a book you read to learn about what happens next in the story. Art can speak about past events, especially historical ones. Stories told by artworks can be also invented.

STREET ART

Art does not belong only to museums or public spaces like parks and squares. You can also find it in the streets of many cities. Images painted with spray paint or stencils are called graffiti. Some feature people, animals, or landscapes, others only letters written in a fancy way. Street artists use walls and pavements to paint their graffiti. Street art can be fun; it is meant to intrigue passersby and make them smile, so the motifs and the way they are painted are selected with humor.

STUDIO

The room in which an artist works and keeps artworks stored until they are completed is called a studio (it can also mean the team assisting an artist). Some artists complete an artwork within one working session, while others make many preparations and spend weeks studying the subject before they create the final work. The size of the studio must be adjusted to the medium; a sculptor will normally need much more space than a painter or a photographer. Also, the equipment varies according to the medium. It is very important that there is enough space for the various objects and tools used by the artist as well as enough light. Natural light is best, so studios tend to have big windows.

STYLE

Each artist has a unique way of creating artworks, of representing things, and of expressing her or his perception of reality. This is called style, and it is similar to handwriting. When you know a bit about art, you can guess who painted, sculpted, or photographed an artwork thanks to the style. You can experience the same with singers – each of them has a different voice and a different way of singing.

SYMBOL

A symbol is a form, an object, or a person that represents an idea or a story. A flag, for instance, is the symbol of a country. Symbols are easily recognizable, like traffic signs. Another example of a symbol could be the alphabet, where letters symbolize the sounds. In art, symbols are widely used. A lion usually symbolizes strength, a dog loyalty. A rose can be a symbol of love; the sun and stars symbolize the sky.

THEME

A theme is the subject of an artwork or a series of artworks. Generally, it is quite easy to find the theme of the work. It is enough to look at it and see what the subject is. In the case of abstract or untitled works, the viewer can decide how they understand the work and what the theme is. It gives you some freedom of interpretation.

TRAVEL

Throughout history artists and craftsmen traveled from city to city, or from country to country, to present their skills and seek new commissions. The most famous and talented ones were invited by great art patrons and royal courts to paint portraits, create sculptures, or construct new buildings. That's how innovation spread across the continents. Nowadays there are many means of promoting one's work, like publications, exhibitions, or the Internet, so now artists travel for inspiration. Many decide to live in various countries for some period of time to learn about new cultures, traditions, and people or to simply experience something different from where they were born and grew up.

TOOLS AND TECHNIQUES

Even within a medium – painting, sculpture, photography – you can see big variations from one artist's work to another's. Each artist not only has their own style, but they also use different techniques and tools. A painter can use specific paints, brushes, and canvasses, and work more or less slowly. On some paintings, the layer of paint is very thin, on others, the artists create style effects with patches of paint. This shows in the final result. Similarly, a photographer may use a particular camera, play with light, select an unusual angle, or focus on a detail, which becomes the focal point.

URBAN

Urban means relating to a city. An urban landscape is a view of a city, be it in a photograph, drawing, or a painting. Urban is also something characteristic of the city or city life. Today, when more and more people on our planet move to big cities, it is very important to design and decorate cities (their districts, parks, or roads) and their architecture in a way that will make living in them pleasant and easy.

TAXI

TAXI

VISIONARIES

If a person has great imagination and original ideas that change the course of history, we call them visionaries. We can find them in various fields and also in the world of art. The most famous artistic visionary was an Italian master of the Renaissance, Leonardo da Vinci, who was not only a brilliant painter and sculptor, but also a very inventive scientist and engineer. To give you an example of his genius, he sketched flying machines five hundred years before the first actual planes!

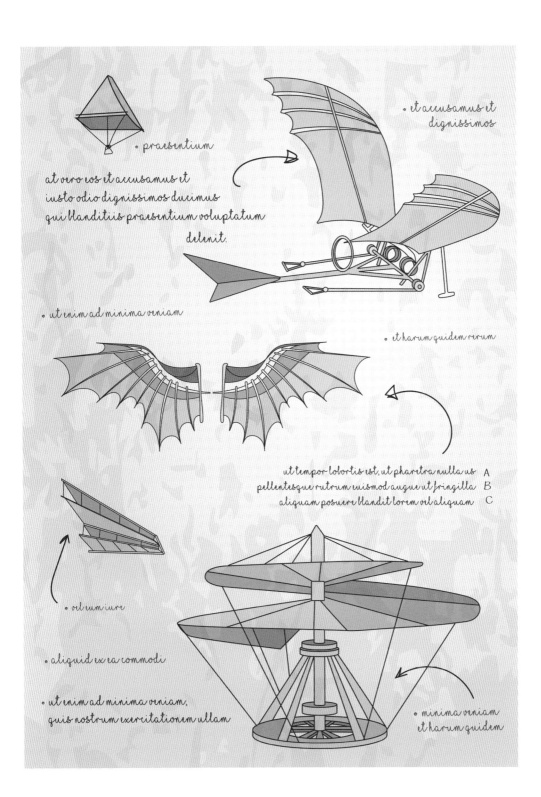

• *praesentium*

• *et accusamus et dignissimos*

at vero eos et accusamus et
iusto odio dignissimos ducimus
qui blanditiis praesentium voluptatum
delenit.

• *ut enim ad minima veniam*

• *et harum quidem rerum*

ut tempor lobortis est, ut pharetra nulla us   A
pellentesque rutrum euismod augue ut fringilla   B
aliquam posuere blandit lorem vel aliquam   C

• *vel eum iure*

• *aliquid ex ea commodi*

• *ut enim ad minima veniam,
quis nostrum exercitationem ullam*

• *minima veniam
et harum quidem*

WORKSHOP

When you like artistic activities like painting, sculpting, or photographing, you can take part in a workshop. It is an educational event organized for a group of people to create their own works and learn something more. Often run by an artist, it usually focuses on a particular technique, medium, or subject.

XXI CENTURY

It is relatively easy to speak about the art of the past. When you know the facts, you can put artworks into chronological or thematic order, and understand their meaning and what role they played in history. It becomes much more difficult with the art of now, because we do not have the necessary distance. But the biggest riddle is the future. How will the coming years of the 21st century change the way artists create art but also the way we see it? There is only one way to learn, namely to keep an eye on what artists do.

Y●U

Art is about interaction between the artist, the artwork, and the viewers. Artists create works of art to express their ideas and emotions. Artworks are rarely created to be kept hidden; they are displayed so that viewers can admire them, appreciate the artists' work, and make up their own mind about them. You can guess the artist's intentions or interpret it in your very own way (the more artworks you know, the better ideas you may come up with). Some contemporary artworks require your direct interaction. Artists invite you to enter specially constructed installations or invent objects that do not work without your presence or movement. By these interesting interactions, you become part of an artwork!

ZEITGEIST

This unusual word comes from German but is used in other languages to describe the spirit of a certain period of time. Whether it is architecture, art, or fashion, each era is characterized by a particular style and ideas that were important at the time. Historical events, significant people, inventions, and developments are all meaningful for the zeitgeist. Our time, for instance, is influenced by new technologies and the Internet, which changed the way we live and create.

CREDITS

Photos Shutterstock: p. 8 © Minii Ho, p. 9, 10 © ANRIR, p. 11 © Macrovector, p. 12 © urfin, p. 13 © Maria Bell, p. 14 left © blossomstar, right © Lera Efremova, p. 15 © baitong333, 16 © Yuriy Vlasenko, 18 © wacomka, 19 © Vector FX, 20 © Clipart deSIGN, 21 © Iconic Bestiary, 22 © imageFlow, 23 © abracada, 24 top © Pretty Vectors, bottom Creative Lab, 25 © muratberkoz, 26 © KUCO, 27 © Anna Marynenko, 28 © forden, 29 © Ildar Galeev, 30 © Graphics4ever, 31 © andersphoto, 32 © ShendArt, 33 © studioworkstock, 34 © Maxx-Studio, 35 © Image Flow, 36 © wjarek, 37 © vectorfusionart, 38, 72 © Morphart Creation, 39 © Tithi Luadthong, 40,41 © stockshoppe, 42 © Lukasz Janyst, 43 © marselparis, 44 top © MaKars, bottom © 5 second Studio, 45 © Orla, 46 © Rafal Gadomski, 47 © Eric Broder Van Dyke, 48-49 © FMonkey Photo, 50 top © FreshPaint, bottom © noreefly, 51 © Kakigori Studio, 52 © Everett – Art, 53 top, 54,55,83,90 © MatiasDelCarmine, bottom left © Visual Generation, bottom right © Jamesbin, 56-57 © Elegant Solution, 58 © Aluna1, 59 © Natalia Ryazantseva, 60-61 © Artishok, 62 © Cat_arch_angel, 63 © Elvetica, 64 ©, berry2046, 65 © Sergey Nivens, 66 © Mastak A, 67 © Panimoni, 69 © filip robert, 70 © simonox, 71 © Rawpixel.com, 73 © Yuliya Koldovska, 74 © Lemonade Serenade, 75 © vanillamilk, 76 © Altagracia Art, 77 top © ecco3d, bottom © kasiastock, 78 © Nicolai Ivanovici, 79 © Tam Patra, 80 © Maria Bo, 81 © SlipFloat, 82 © lora pi, 84 top © MSSA, bot-tom © Denis Maliugin, 85 © mazura1989, 86 © tanyaya, 87 © Mix3r, 88-89 © KPG Ivary, 91 © Kwirry, 92 © elenabsl, 93 © turbodesign, 94 © Reamolko, 95 © iurii.

Created by:

FANCY BOOKS

www.fancy-books-packaging.com

© Agata & Pierre Toromanoff / Fancy Books Packaging
© For this edition Eken Press Ltd. 2017

Copyediting: Rebecca Packard
Layout & Cover Design: Fancy Books Packaging

Printed in Estonia, 2017

ISBN 978-1-908233-02-8

Eken Press Ltd. is a company registered in England and Wales under the number 7454591. Follow us on ekenpress.com.